To Sally
With love and
    gratitude for your
        friendship
            Kate x

Linda Peters

Reflections of the Light

First published in Great Britain in 2022 by Happy Life Publishing

Copyright © 2022 by Kathalyn Hamilton & Linda Peters
Cover Image by Linda Peters
Formatting by The Amethyst Angel

Interior artwork and photographs by
Linda Peters
Hazel Burridge
Katy Jones

ISBN: 978-1-7391125-0-9

First Edition

REFLECTIONS OF THE LIGHT

Channellings by

KATHALYN HAMILTON

Illustrations by

LINDA PETERS

This book is for all the Light Workers & Earth Angels across the world.

Acknowledgements

First and foremost we would like to send so much love and gratitude to our Spirit Guides, Joseph and Rama, for making this book possible and for their patience and encouragement.

Thanks also to the wonderful Michelle Gordon, the Earth Angel who helped us so much with her advice and knowledge to bring this book into being.

Love and gratitude to Roger and Beryl for their endless work for Spirit at the Point of Light, and for introducing Linda and myself at one of their development circles.

Thank you to all our friends for their encouragement and to Annie for giving us the title of the book.

Thank you to Katy and Hazel for their amazing contributions and to our beautiful Mother Earth who has shared her beauty and strength with us throughout our lives.

FOREWORD

This book is long overdue and I am very glad that it here at last. I have known the two authors (Kathalyn and Linda) for many, many years and I am honoured to list them among my friends.

Kathalyn is a excellent medium, astrologer and healer. During the many years that I have known her, I have seen Kathalyn bloom as a spiritual medium and I have been aware of her channeling Joseph since early 2017. Joseph has been an inspiration for many on the Earth Plane. He has a knack for expressing Eternal Truth in a simple way that allows us all to understand and grow closer to the Great Spirit. Many people have found inspiration, hope and help from Joseph's words and I am very glad that at last we can find them all in one place.

I have also known Linda for many years and she is an amazing artist. I am very honoured that I have one of her original paintings of Archangel Rafael hanging on my living room wall. Linda is an exceptionally talented artist and her mediumistic skills have enabled her to bring many pictures through from the realms of Spirit. Pictures that have inspired many people and brought the reality of Spirit to all that have seen her work. I have often sat and watched as Linda has linked with spirit and brought through drawings of people's loved ones that are now in the spirit realm. Her channeling is fast and accurate and has brought joy to many.

It is a sign of their love for others that Kathalyn and Linda have included work from two other friends, Katy and Hazel, in this book.

This book is a really excellent work of art that will bring its readers closer to the Great Spirit. Joseph's words bring messages of hope, love and peace at a time when this world finds itself in so much turmoil.

I have no hesitation in recommending this book to you. May Light and Love and Peace be with you all.

Roger Beer, July 2022.

Introduction

For many years now Linda and I have been working together giving private readings and working in local churches as platform mediums. While Joseph will send through his messages, Linda will channel her spirit art from her Guide Rama. The idea for this book has come to us gradually with a few hiccups along the way, but we hope you will enjoy both the spirit art and the messages of love and hope.

We are so lucky to have had some more wonderful spirit art given to us for this book by Katy Jones and Hazel Burridge. Linda has also contributed some messages of love and wisdom from her guides. So as you can see, we have gathered inspiration from many light sources.

When you turn the pages of this book your eyes will be drawn to the words and the paintings that will resonate with you at that time. Know that you also have your own guides who are waiting patiently for you to become aware of their presence and their love.

When you feel lost and alone we hope you will pick up this book and find comfort.

All our love,
Linda and Kathalyn

Joseph

CONTENTS

Love Grows Stronger When You Give It Away

Love is a gift of Light placed in the palm of your hand.

It is so beautiful that you want to share it, to give it away to others.

The more you give it away, the stronger it gets, it never ends, it is never used up.

It is the only thing that by giving it away you end up having more and more.

Healing is love

Compassion is giving love.

Standing beside another in their time of trial is giving love.

Never be afraid you will run out of love. The small light in the palm of your hand will grow to encompass your whole being

The more you give it away.

All blessings,
Joseph

TIME

Many of you feel that time is slipping away from you, there is just not enough of it and so you are continually trying to grasp it to achieve all you wish to do. There is no greater disturber to peace of mind than the rush to fit desired objectives into limited time. So we would say, allow the illusion of time to settle around you like a gentle exhaling of a deep breath. The more you chase it the more elusive it becomes. Relax into each moment and time will expand and you will be able to achieve all you wish to do.

The energies of your planet have accelerated with the onset of so many electronic devices. This energy, while necessary in your earth time now and beneficial in many ways, is all around you. It cannot be seen, but it speeds up the illusion of time, giving the sensation of rushing to catch up. Take a deep breath, focus on the moment, the task that you are performing, and you will feel an inner peace, a slowing down of urgency that will lessen the tension and stress that is so prevalent in your world today.

All blessings,
Joseph

Artwork by Hazel Burridge

The Tale of the Silver Coin

I was standing in the darkness, the pitch black.

I could not see a thing.

Then I noticed, shining on the ground, a little silver coin.

I picked it up and its light enabled me to see around.

Standing near me was a person also in the dark, so I handed them my coin to light up their darkness.

To my surprise I still had my coin, I still had my light, but now there were two of us.

Then we could see another person suffering in the dark, so we handed them the glowing coin.

This is how it went, the silver coin travelling from person to person, getting brighter and brighter until there was no more darkness.

Never be afraid to give away your light, it will only shine brighter for you and everyone who receives it. Keep it only to illumine your own darkness and it will tarnish.

Pass it on and it will light the whole world.

All blessings,
Joseph

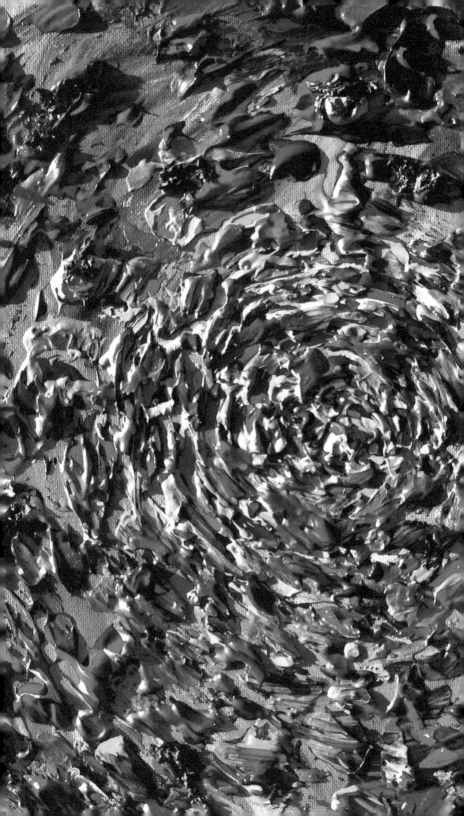

When You Feel You Are Going Round In Circles

You may sometimes feel in your earth life you are going round and round in circles. In truth this is not so. We can see that your lives are like spirals, each circle taking you upwards, closer to the light.

Never give up hope, you are moving forwards, always progressing even when times are dark. We are always with you, just a breath away, and if you reach out your hands we will take them and give you strength.

You are never alone, remember this, you are a Light Worker, part of a wonderful group bringing Light to the earth plane where it is most needed.

All blessings,
Joseph

The Power of the Mind

The mind is infinite, there are no boundaries to the mind, and your thoughts are the instruments that shape the mind. Thought is all powerful, it can turn heaven to hell or hell into heaven. This is why it is so important to teach yourself to attach your thoughts to that which is positive and constructive and of the Light.

Imagine if you will, a beautiful tower, fragile yet strong, reaching into the clear skies. You can climb this tower and look with wonder over the lands beneath you, full of light and beauty. Close by is a woodland, the trees grow close together, it is dark and forbidding. Yet there is a path going through the woods that can be taken. This is like the mind. Your thoughts can take you up into the light or into the dark forest.

However the important thing to remember is that you can always leave the darkness of the forest, the Light is always waiting for you. This is why it is so important to train your thoughts. It is not easy, and it does not happen overnight; but little by little you can catch your thoughts when they wander towards the dark forest and bring them back towards the land of the Light. We are always there to help you. We do not want you to be fearful and full of doubt, this is not the way of Spirit.

So do not feel helpless, for you have the power to turn your thoughts around and each step you take makes it easier. The first steps are the most difficult, but once you take them we join arms with you. Never lose hope, never give in to fear, you are so much greater than you can possibly imagine. You carry infinite wisdom and knowing within you. The blanket of doubt and fear that sometimes covers this is only an illusion, it is not reality.

Keep faith with Light and truth and beauty despite the darkness around you in the world. The Light will always win, it is of your Creator, the very Source of all life and every living being.

8

Free Will & Karma

Many of you wonder about free will and karma. Do you have free will? Or is it just the treadmill of karma, repaying past debts, while hoping for a better future? We would like to reassure you that you hold your lives in your own hands. This is wonderful and awe inspiring, but also can be quite intimidating.

Every decision you make paves the way for your future, and this is what karma is all about. It is not some committee deciding you owe certain debts that have to be repaid. Each one of you has the opportunity to create the life you want by your actions, your thoughts and your decisions. Time is continuous, it does not start and finish, so your path may go forwards from earth life to earth life should you chose to incarnate again.

Let us reassure you that free will and karma are the same thing. It is your free will that creates your karma. Is this not wonderful? For you can always create a better future, you can always learn, always progress. There is no Almighty Judge meting our merits or punishments. Each one of us decides our own future from life to life.

So grasp each opportunity with both hands, do not be scared, always try to live by the Light, by Compassion and Kindness. It does not matter what mistakes you have made in the past, think only about how you act and react today. Make it your best day, and then it will be your best tomorrow as well.

All blessings,
Joseph

RESENTMENT

Resentment is a familiar feeling for many, and one which you often wish you did not have. It is one of those emotions you think you have conquered which comes back when you are not looking.

Resentment comes from the feeling you have not been treated fairly, or when others have wronged or misunderstood you. The danger is that resentment gives rise to the misunderstanding that other people are responsible for how you feel, that it is their fault, they have caused the problem or distress. How often do you hear a person blaming their parents for the way they are, or for what is wrong in their lives? If not parents, it is the husband or the wife, or even the government. Resentment can eat away at you without bringing any benefit at all to yourself or to the other. It is a very hard emotion to control.

However look at it in a different way. We incarnate in groups, each one agreeing before incarnation to help the other with the lesson or karma they need to progress forwards. Maybe in this life, you needed to learn greater self reliance, to trust more in your own judgement, and so you incarnated to parents who were often absent, or unable to be there for you. Do not blame them for your difficulties, but thank them for the opportunities they have given you to grow stronger.

This is the crux of the matter, my friend. All life experiences are an opportunity to grow in understanding, in strength and in love. Sometimes it is the most difficult people in our lives who teach us the most. This could be the agreement you had together before incarnation, the thorn in your side is the one who is there to help you with tolerance, patience and love. We are not saying you should allow yourself to be badly treated, as self respect is vital. You are a diving being in essence. If resentment occurs, move on, let go, know that you have completed the karma and are starting a new chapter in your life.

All blessings, Joseph

Forgiveness

We have spoken to you about resentment and now we would like to offer you the antidote to resentment, which is forgiveness. To forgive not only those who have wronged you, but to forgive yourself, and perhaps this is the hardest thing to do. You are willing to give love and compassion to others, but often withhold it from yourselves. Why is this? Do you not feel you are worthy of Love? Do you not feel that you deserve to be forgiven?

How can you separate your own well-being from those around you, are you not all children of God, part of the Divine Spirit? Each of you is as important as the person standing next to you, there is no difference. Once you learn to forgive yourself, to accept your shortcomings, to nurture your own well-being, you will find it easier to forgive others.

How can you judge yourself, or your brothers and sisters, when you cannot see the whole picture? You only see the aspect of the picture that affects you personally. Know that you are so loved from this plane of living because you try so hard. We see your courage, we see you efforts to be true to the Light and we love you for this. Never judge yourselves, be kind, not only to other people, but to yourself also. Be gentle, for there is greater strength in sincere kindness than in judgement and outspokenness.

All blessings,
Joseph

Artwork by Linda Peters

LOVING KINDNESS

Remember that people are not all that they appear to be, they are merely acting out the appropriate role for this incarnation. The man begging on the street corner with his dog, is not a beggar in his heart, he has chosen this clothing to help him with his spiritual development.

This is hard to believe, I know. Who would chose such a humiliating and uncomfortable incarnation? In the spirit planes, earth life is so short, it is just the blink of an eye, and so we all decided to undertake uncomfortable incarnations that we felt would help us grow towards the Light.

You interact with each other in order to learn compassion, tolerance and love, the greatest spiritual lessons. Try to see past the outer clothing of a person to their spiritual being. To the hardships they have undertaken, to the love they have been denied in their earth life, to the pain of their physical body. View all those around you with the eyes of Spirit, without judgement, with compassion and kindness.

We cannot speak too highly of kindness. It is the gentle reaching out of Love towards another soul, answering their needs without judgement or intolerance. You are all on a journey, all are needing a helping hand, so reach out to each other, link arms in support. Each has a destiny, each has lessons to learn, potential to fulfil. You are all of the same spirit, all from the same Great and Wonderful Source.

All blessings,
Joseph

Artwork by Linda Peters

Be Yourself

You have not been put on this earth to be like anyone else, or to put it another way, you did not chose to incarnate in this life to learn anyone's lessons but your own. There will always be other people you wish to emulate, who seem to have a better life, who have greater talents, who have the answers to problems. It is tempting to copy them, to try to ease your way through life by walking in the footsteps of someone else.

However, you are unique. Your way of living, your gifts, and your destiny is unique. You cannot learn your lessons by looking at anyone else. You cannot grow by emulating the growth of another.

Do not compare yourself to other people, they have their own path, just as you have yours. Be truly yourself, work always to overcome weaknesses, to unfold your potential, to express your talents and beliefs. Be confident in who you are, you are a Child of God, you are unique and wonderful. You do not need to be like anyone else, only to express, to the best of your ability, your true being which is the potential of your Spirit.

Most important is that you do not judge yourself. As we have said before, you cannot see the whole picture. Be gentle and loving towards yourself as you would be towards others that you love.

FEAR

Fear is part of the human condition, and it can take many forms. Fear of pain, of death, of humiliation or failure, you have all experienced fear in one form or another. We would say that fear comes from the thought of losing something that is valued, be it possessions, health, a loved one, or even life itself. When you incarnate into earth life you forget how strong you are, you forget your spirit is eternal and can suffer no loss. It is only the physical material vibrations that can be taken away from you.

The more you become aware of your spiritual reality while on earth, the less grip fear can have on you. You will realise that even if the worst you can imagine occurs, your true reality will still be intact, and will be for eternity. Is this not an amazing thought? Nothing can destroy you, you are an Eternal Being, loved completely by your Creator.

20

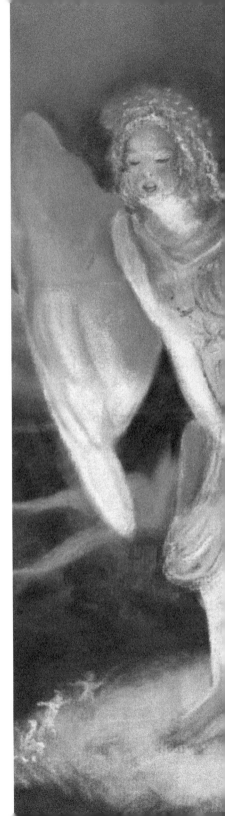

Fears often come in unspecified form, they lurk at the corners of your mind, casting a shadow over you. Turn around and face that fear, shine the light upon it, do not allow it to take hold. Say to your fear, "I see you, I acknowledge you." Do not try to hide away from it or be intimidated by it. In truth, you are stronger than any fear, and when you face whatever is troubling you, you become stronger and stronger.

See life as an adventure, do not try to hide away from your fears and stay safe. There are lessons to be learnt and experiences to travel through, and you know you will always come safely through to the other side. How can you not? Even death from your world leads to the greater joy of our Spirit World.

My friend, look fear in the face when it comes calling, and know in your heart that you will be able to cope with whatever comes towards you in your earth life.

Fear, once generated, is catching. It can spread like wildfire, and can even generate that which is feared. Take for example the fear of war. If this seed is planted in the minds of the population it can become powerful enough to bring about enmity and strife.

So too can a calm and loving outlook spread to those around you. Thought is tangible even though unseen, thoughts of Love will bring peace, thoughts of fear and loss can bring war. But I stray to another subject, another strand of thought, so I will leave you with all blessings of Love.

All blessings, Joseph

JOSEPH

We have talked together many times now, and I am glad that these words have brought some measure of comfort and Light to you and others. It may be that you would like to know more about my identity, my past incarnations and life purposes while on Earth. However it is not as relevant as my purpose and work now, which is to teach, to spread an understanding of the truths of Spirit, the Love of Spirit, and to help you to understand that you are all surrounded by Love.

You may see me as a teacher of Love. How strange this sounds, as if I were an agony aunt in one of your magazines. Perhaps I do not explain myself well. In your world there is much confusion, caused by a concentration on the physical and material aspects of life. So we try, from our world, to bring a balance, to present to you Spiritual Truths, a glimpse of the true reality of life, of which you are a part.

We try to remind you that however difficult your life is on earth, however confusing, you are walking towards

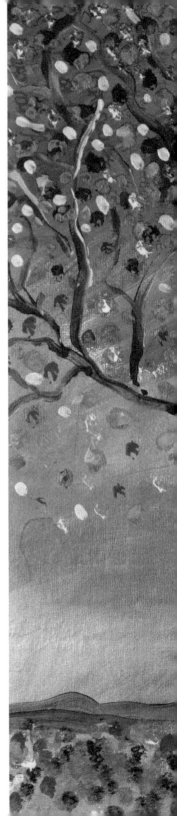

Artwork by Linda Peters

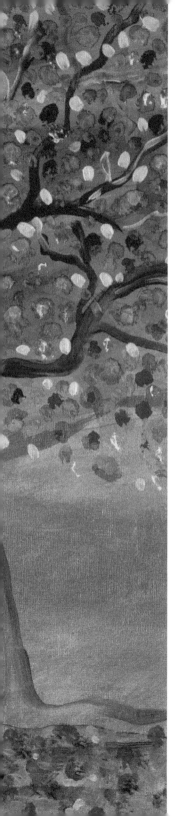

the Light. You are in temporary residence on the earth plane, working through issues that have clouded your Light, and most important, that you have chosen to work through. There is no stern headmaster that has sent you to this earth life to learn your lessons, you have chosen to return, to overcome difficulties, and to help others so that you may all grow closer to the Light of Love and Joy.

Be kind to yourself, be kind to each other, be your own best friend. Your earth life is but a short span and you have incarnated with all the tools and abilities you need to progress and to work through the difficulties that present themselves.

You have been born with an understanding of your particular destiny, and all that you need to fulfil that destiny.

Do not doubt yourself, you are so much stronger, and so much greater, than you can possibly imagine.

All blessings,
Joseph

Accepting Yourself

Do not try to escape from an awareness of what you consider to be your weaknesses. You are not expected to be perfect, you are experiencing earth life which is by its very nature flawed. Your weaknesses are stepping stones to greater strength and wisdom and as such need to be accepted not hidden with a feeling of shame.

When you feel you have fallen short of your own expectations, look with clear eyes at the pattern of behaviour and accept it as part of your growth. We ask that you love your weaknesses as you would a small child that is learning to walk or to speak.

Once you accept yourself, you will find it so much easier to look at other people with love, despite the mistakes they make. Because how you treat yourself will be how you look at the world around you. It is easier to recognise behaviour patterns in others that we have ourselves (I too, have walked the earth, remember) and sometimes we escape looking at ourselves by concentrating on the weaknesses of another. However, all is one, all are linked as we often say, so to offer love and understanding to another is to offer it also to yourself.

Always look things in the eye, they will make you stronger and bring greater tolerance.

All blessings,
Joseph

Light Workers

We speak a lot about light workers, and sometimes you must wonder what the qualifications are to become a light worker, and what it really means. The Truth is quite simple, a light worker is one who carries love in their hearts towards every living being. Towards all those they meet on their earth journey: people, animals, all of nature and Mother Earth. It is an energy of the heart that streams forth caring and kindness towards others.. This love is a reflection of the love of the Great Spirit. You are carrying a reflection of His Love for all creation and so you are a lightworker.

Light and Love cannot be separated, they vibrate with the same energy. We do not expect you in your earth life to be able to send forth Light all the time, for you are human, and you have incarnated with the restrictions of physical life. But we would say it is the *intention* here that is important. When you have the intention to help, to love, to heal, then that is enough. If this is what motivates your actions then your light will grow stronger. If your intention is pure, though at times misguided, then you are truly giving your best to be a light worker. You may be misunderstood and sometimes criticized, but if your intention is for good, this is protection for you.

Do not worry about being criticized or misunderstood. If you are true to your own heart, to what you feel to be right, then you are following the right path for you. You are living by your own light, and this is important. Sometimes you may be persuaded against your better judgement, but do not worry about this. In retrospect, you will be able to see your mistake, and this is a valuable lesson for the future.

Again I have strayed from the original purpose of our talk, but it is all relevant. There is so much to say and yet in some ways it is all so simple. Be kind, be true to the light within you and you cannot go wrong.

All blessings, Joseph

A Waterfall Of Light

When you look at the world around you, the problems, the suffering and the ignorance can seem so great; you can despair that you cannot make a difference. You feel so small, so insignificant, and the problems of your world so large, so deep rooted. What could you possibly do?

And yet, imagine yourself as a small stream of water running down a mountain, almost insignificant in the enormity of the mountains, but there are other small streams also pouring down off the mountains. These join together forming a river, then a torrent, and finally a great waterfall of light, charging the air and the land with golden light energy. So it is with you. You might feel small and insignificant in your efforts to bring Light to your world, but you are not alone. The combined power of the light each person holds is magnificent. And consider the numerous others like you throughout the world, imagine the wonderful combined power of the light each of you sends forth to help those in need, to replenish the earth, to heal those in distress.

It is wonderful to see from our world, truly wonderful. So never give up. Continue to send forth the Light, to offer love and kindness wherever you go. The whole vibration of your planet will glow with light with the combined efforts of all our cherished light workers.

We thank you all
All blessings
Joseph

Your Mindset

The mindset you carry now is the same mindset you will take with you into the spirit world. This is why it is so important to live with an appreciation of all that you have, and all that you experience in your world now.

If you feel hard done by, full of resentment and anger, this mindset will not change when you reach our world because it is all you will see. It is so important for you to realise that your thoughts create your world, they are the magnet that shapes your life.

Do not think that everything will automatically be sorted when you reach our world. Indeed your physical ailments will no longer be with you, but you will not become a different person. Always look to the good, to the blessings that surround you, to the kindness you give and receive. In this way you are walking in the Light, and this is what you will carry forwards. You are attuning with the spark of inner light within you, and this is the reality, even the currency, in our world.

All blessings,
Joseph

Do Not Put Us on a Pedestal

Do not put us on a pedestal. Do not feel we are greater beings set apart from you, who may or may not come to your assistance when requested. We are always with you, we are not far removed, and while our vision may be wider because we are not limited by the dense vibrations of earth, we too are on our own spiritual journey. Without you we could not work. We share a common purpose of service to the Light, and bringing love and tolerance and understanding into the world.

Talk to us as you would your best friends, never feel you are separated or not good enough. We have all passed along the road you are travelling and wish only to make your journey easier and to bring you greater understanding of your true purpose, and the greatness of your being.

Blessings,
Joseph

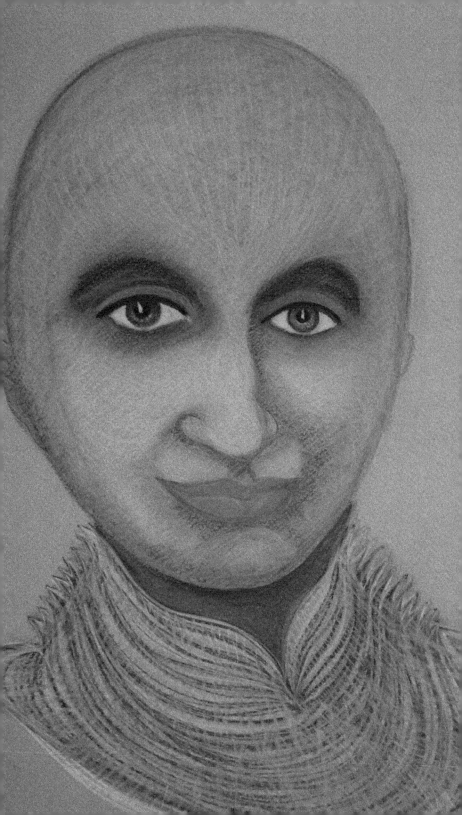

SERVICE

The word *service* in your world does not always have good connotations, rather it is a dry word linked to repsonsibility and sometimes boredom. Servants were known to be 'in service', you have civil servants, you have a church service, you even have 'servers' at the food table. And yet the path of service is glorious, it is an adventure, full of light and joy. Think for a minute of your essence, do you not come from the great creative spark of love? And what could be more fulfilling than to work with the energy source from which you were created?

The path is not smooth, it is often challenging, but the rewards, and the satisfaction is immense. It is like finding your way after wandering around in the shade, it is a feeling of 'rightness'.

You may ask 'What is service?' and we would say it is living your life as an expression of all that you know to be good and loving.

To see all created life as an extension of yourself, as an integral part of you, so that you treat everything and everyone as you would wish to be treated. It is that somple. Everything is linked, we tell you this often, so whatever you give forth you give also to yourself, there is no distinction.

All blessings,
Joseph

The Diamond Of Many Facets

The life you are living now is just a fragment of your true reality. Imagine a lustrous, many-faceted diamond.

Bright, shining and clear light.

This is your true reality.

When you incarnate is it as if you have chosen to polish one of the facets of this diamond. As we often say, you are so much greater, so much more powerful than you can ever imagine. The life you are expressing now is but a small part that you have chosen to work on to refine and bring to greater brightness.

Through the times you are living now, you are exploring your greater reality, your awareness in increasing, and although this can be unsettling it is also wonderful to experience more of your true reality while still on earth. Do not be afraid, you are held safe in our love, you cannot fall, we hold you close.

All blessings,
Joseph

YOU ARE A MIGHTY SPIRIT

You are a Mighty Spirit. Never lose sight of this. We understand your daily life on earth involves much organisation, many matters to attend to, but never let yourself lose sight of your greatness, your ability to step away from your physical material life into your true reality.

You share this reality with all living expressions of matter around you, so you are not alone, but linked to a glorious whole that is not limited by time or space.

Step outside of your daily concerns, these will pass, whatever they may be. Become aware of the glorious reality that you share with the created universe and beyond.

On earth, you are all brothers and sisters, for you come from the same spiritual parentage, your divine spark is shared with all that surrounds you both in our world and in yours.

There is no separation in Truth, just different expressions of the Creative Source of All, and this is Love

S.B.

Source Energy

All things are contained within the energy of the universe, it is the source of all, there is nothing that does not have its origin in this Source Energy. No one on your earth has the ability or receptivity to align with all the myriad aspects of the source, it is too great and the nature of earth is limitation.

However, according to your gifts, your potential and your experience you are able to tune in to the energy of the source to which you are attuned. For example through art, through words, through scientific knowledge, through love and healing.

Source energy is power, and it is for you to use it as befits your receptivity in this incarnation.

Choose always to direct this power towards that which is uplifting, that can better the lives of those who share your world. There is always the choice, the power is in your hands to lift and heal, to bring light and peace or to turn your back on the opportunity.

Know and own your power and use it for the greater good. However small the thought, the gesture, or the creation, it is important and will effect the whole.

S.B

Artwork by Linda Peters

Spiritual DNA

You are aware of your physical DNA, but are you also aware that each of you has a spiritual DNA that links you to your soul group and to your Spirit Guides and helpers?

How is this spiritual DNA formed? It is from your spiritual family, those with whom you have incarnated over many lifetimes and who have given their allegiance to each other to help them spiritually.

Your soul group is like your spiritual family, and consists of beings on different stages of their spiritual journey. We use the word 'being' because a group may contain Angels, beings from another planet and other manifestations of life. You may feel very drawn to some people you have never met before, and this is often a recognition that they are part of your spirit group.

This is why kindness and empathy is so important because you have all agreed to help each other on your spiritual journey.

All blessings,
Joseph

LONELY

Great Spirit, Higher Self, Angels and Spirit Guides, what guidance and words of wisdom do you have for our people today?

'Message for the lonely.'

We are coming to you today with the enfoldance of love and concern and to suggest that each and every one of you embraces every minute of your time on Earth.

We are always with you, helping, supporting and loving each and every one of you. You are never alone, Dear One. We are here to help.

If your thoughts turn to despair, remember that we are here with you, enfolding you in our wings of love and giving you, gently, the strength to carry on. It is often in your darkest moments on earth that we feel closer to you and are carrying you. So fear not, Dear One, we are here and we love you. Amen.

Channelled by Linda Peters
21 May 2021

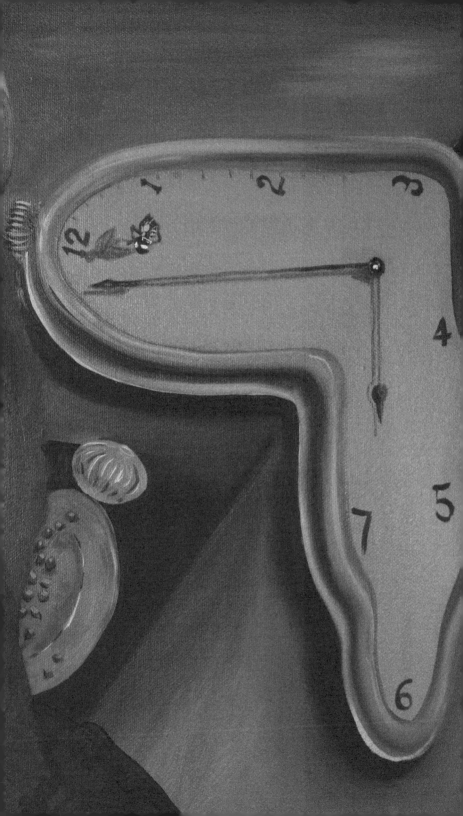

Signs

In days gone by signs would be left along a track or pathway to guide those following behind. An arrow in the dirt, a broken twig, a feather from a bird. These were left as signs to guide.

In the same way, we give you signs to help you along your spiritual path, and these can vary. For some of you it is numbers, for others birds, sometimes the written or spoken word. You have all experienced these things.

The trick is to be aware, to extend your consciousness so that these signs do not go unnoticed for they are there to reassure and guide you.

Step out side of your busy mind and look around, there is guidance always when you have sent forth a request. Your prayers are always answered, it is for you to listen and be aware.

All blessings,
Joseph

Meditation

We know there are many of you who meditate and sit in peace, often daily. This is wonderful because it is the time when we can draw close to you and commune with you. However we understand there is much concern about the right way to meditate and frustration when you feel you have not achieved stillness of the mind.

It is the nature of thoughts to be active, and so the secret is not to engage with them. You cannot stop thoughts with more thoughts. So allow them their freedom. It is the nature of your consciousness that is important, not the control of your thoughts. Be aware of the light, the love that surrounds you, feel this in your heart, in your core being and the thoughts will take care of themselves.

When you feel you have wandered away from this awareness gently bring yourself back. Do not feel you have failed in any way. All meditation is good, there in not perfect way to meditate, know that the light of spirit is with you, and relax into it.

All blessings,
Joseph

Spirit See The Light In Your Heart

You are very aware of your shortcomings, of your little ways and idiosyncrasies, and you feel these are important in your struggle towards the light. We would reassure you that we see only the desire of the heart, this is what shines forth to us. Where there is the desire of the heart to serve, to bring forwards the energy of love to your earth life, this is what we see and what we can work with.

You have an awareness of where and when you have tripped up, do not dwell on these, know that to us here in spirit we see the light that shines from your heart and this is what brings us close to you.

Judgement is based on fear, leave it behind both for yourself and for others, see only the goodness and kindness that is being offered, however it is expressed

All blessings,
Joseph

Hope For The Future

There is always hope for the future. Even when you are going through times of trial, when all seems dark and unfriendly, there is a better future ahead. Everything is transitory, there is always the light of hope leading you on, like a lantern being held up in the darkness for you.

Many of you have lost your faith in the future, you are going through the motions, but joy and happiness seem beyond your grasp. Keep faith, there is light coming over the horizon always. Even when you are leaving this earth life, there is a better life ahead of you.

You are an eternal being, there is always a future and there is always the light and love of spirit waiting for you, and if you will accept it around you now, every minute of your life.

All blessings,
Joseph

Ascension Path

You have been told from many sources about the Ascension Path, about 3 dimensional energy and 5 dimensional energy and these things can be confusing to you. They cause doubt as to whether you are doing the right thing or are on the right path, and make you wonder if you are good enough.

We would say to rest your mind. The Ascension path is one you have been on since you incarnated, indeed from even before this. It is the path of your soul, your spirit, it is not something new and no one can suddenly jump on this path. It is an unfolding of what is already within you.

The energies at this time are lighting up all that is occurring and this is what you are seeing and feeling. Everything is being exposed, the Light is stronger and the darkness is no longer hidden.

You made your choice to follow the Light, to act with kindness and love wherever possible, to be true to your spirit and this is what is taking you forwards. Know that you are completely safe, that whatever occurs, life is eternal, you are surrounded by the wings of Angels. Nothing is stronger than the light and this is what will guide you.

All blessings,
Joseph

The Intelligence Of Mother Earth

Never underestimate the intelligence of your planet. All the physical expressions of energy that manifest are linked together by an amazing network of intelligence that does not take into account time or space. What occurs in the ocean in one continent is felt and understood by the trees in another continent. This may be hard for you to accept, but it is so. Nothing occurs in the natural world of your planet that is not registered throughout all expressions of natural life.

So many dwell on the surface of this magnificence without any conception of the wonder of the network of intelligence upon which they are living. But understand that you are also part of this, you do not have to be disconnected, you too carry the same creative spark of being.

Respect all forms of life, you are all linked, everything has energy vibrations, a tree crashing to the ground in one country is felt by the forests the other side of the world. It is a wonder to respect and love.

All blessings,
Joseph

Photo by Linda Peters

Turn Your Thoughts from Fear to Upliftment

You may feel sometimes that we talk always of love and the light that streams down towards you from the Spirit World. What about all the disasters on earth? What about the cruelty, the greed, the lack of respect for other living beings? Do we in spirit live in a place removed from the awareness of all strife? In truth, we focus with you on the power of love, on the energy of light, because it lifts the entire vibration of your planet.

We are completely aware of the dark side of life, but we wish to turn your thoughts towards that which is positive, is beneficial and uplifting, not that which will darken the energy of life on your planet even further. If each one of you on earth turns your face towards the light, towards the actions of love and wisdom, the light around you shines brighter and brighter. This in itself will weaken the tide of upset and strife.

The more people that turn towards Good, towards tolerance and kindness, the weaker the darkness becomes. Do not live in fear, in despair at what is occurring at this present time. Life on your planet has always been this way.

Link yourselves with the great tide of light, of the higher energy vibrations that are available to you. As we always say to you, the light is stronger than any darkness

All blessings,
Joseph

Stand Still & Get Your Bearings

Sometimes you just need to stand still and get your bearings. There is such pressure in your world to be always doing, always moving forwards, always being in control, that sometimes the way forwards is lost.

When things become overwhelming and you feel you are always trying to catch up with time, just stop, just be still and allow things to settle around you. In this way you will be able to see what is important and what is superficial and can be left.

Remember, perfection is not expected. People are more important than chores and your well-being is the most important concern for you. This is not selfish, it is vital that you care for yourself. You are not the myriad demands of your life, let them go if only for a few minutes. Focus on what really matters, take a deep breath, become aware and rest in that moment.

All blessings,
Joseph

Artwork by Katy Jones

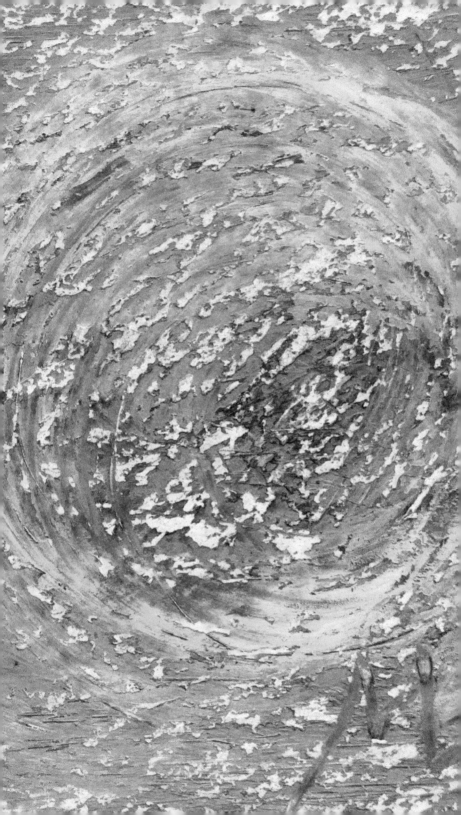

Your Divine Spark

When you are born, you carry the divine spark within you. As you grow in earth years this spark gradually becomes subdued beneath layers of conditioning to the material world. What is happening now to many is that the creative spark of light is trying to break through the crust that has been built up over the years of your life.

This can be uncomfortable and unsettling, but it is worth the struggle. It is a time of awakening for many people, so allow yourself to relax in the process. Know that your inner light is answering a call to be recognised and expressed. You will be drawn to like minded people so you may all help each other. Our light army on earth.

All blessings,
Joseph

Corruption & Lies Can No Longer Be Hidden

You may feel that your emotions are fluctuating greatly at this time and this is a reflection of the energies around you all now. On a national and global scale, corruption and lies are being exposed. What has been hidden is rising to the surface and this is causing ripples that are being felt everywhere and unsettling the energies of your planet. No longer will presenting an acceptable surface be enough, it is a time for truth to become apparent.

You may find this in your personal life, events from the past keep coming to the surface and disturbing your peace of mind. Do not fight them, accept them as part of your journey and allow them to take their place. You have moved on and the experiences and decisions have given you the knowledge you needed.

Above all, know that what is occurring is a cleansing both on a global and a personal level. There has been too much emphasis on correct presentation rather than the reality of what lies beneath the surface. Truth will not be hidden.

All blessings,
Joseph

Artwork by Linda Peters

Your Guardian Angel

We wish to remind you that you have a Guardian Angel close with you at all times. You are never alone, you are never without love. Accept your Guardian Angel into your awareness, allow them to come close, for they cannot help you in so strong a manner if you do not allow them to enter your consciousness.

As with all life, it is your acceptance, your awareness, that brings you into alignment and allows you to be helped, to be guided. While you may accept truth intellectually, it is the acceptance of the heart that allows the love of spirit to come close.

Be constantly aware of our closeness, of our love and this will allow us to merge with your earth life, and to give you guidance and support. We are here with love, but we need you to accept us.

Talk with us we are with you constantly, simply a word, or a thought away.

All blessings,
Joseph

Relationships (1)

When you look back over the relationships in your life, or even those in your present time, do not think about them in terms of success or failure, disappointment or fulfilment. Look at them with gratitude for the greater understanding they have brought you. We speak here of all relationships, friendships, partners, parents and children and work colleagues. There is more wisdom to be gained from the experience of relationships than in any other way.

Have you been hurt or let down? Do not blame the other person, but instead recognise it as an opportunity to learn, to grow in understanding. It will have been arranged between you and them before incarnation that there would be a coming together and interaction between you. Both parties will be learning and growing, the important thing is to treat each other with respect and kindness no matter what is occurring. We could say so much on this subject. It may be that the other person is helping to strengthen your boundaries, to teach self love, or to help you fulfil your potential. Be open to the opportunities for development that you are being given.

Nothing is random, do not criticise yourself for the choices you have made, all are relevant, all are for your greater good. Do not hang onto injustices or hurt, but acknowledge what has happened and move forwards as a stronger person.

All blessings,
Joseph

Artwork by Linda Peters

Relationships (2)

We would like to talk with you more about relationships. As you are aware, most of your close relationships are with those of your own soul group. This is because there has been an agreement made before incarnation to help each other with your spiritual progress. However, once lessons have been learned it may be then time for one or the other to move along their particular path. By relationships, we mean friendships, family, partners and work colleagues. Just because there is a karmic connection, it does not mean that there is no flexibility and that things are set in stone.

It is not advisable to stay in a connection where you are losing your self respect. At this point it may be that the lesson being given is to stand in your own power and move forwards. However, some connections are ended because of boredom or the chance of something more exciting. Then it is likely there is still much to learn and to be gained from the relationship.

Hard to tell the difference? Look into your heart, listen to your intuition, is there a response from the one with whom you are in connection or is there a continual drain on your energy? All relationships need to be shared, there must be giving and receiving from both sides.

This is a deep and important subject, and there is no magic code or answer. Each relationship is completely different because of the karma that is brought forwards by each of you. Why have we not mentioned Love? The love is there in the agreement of the two people to incarnate at the same period of time and to help each other evolve spiritually and emotionally. Cruelty is never acceptable in any form. While it is important to look at the needs of the person with whom you are in connection, it is also important to look at your own needs. Do not give your power away, stand tall in your beliefs and give the other person the respect and space to hold their own beliefs and opinions.

Artwork by Linda Peters

We will leave this here for now, but we will talk again on this subject. There is more to be learned from relationships, from the interaction between you than in any other way. All relationships are precious, even those that have caused you hurt and have given you strength.

All blessings, Joseph

Relationships (3)

When a relationship ends or a friendship seems to fade away, do not be sad or hurt. It will be because the contract between you has come to an end. The help and love you agreed to give to each other for your spiritual journeys will have been achieved and you both need to move forwards.

Where loss is caused by one returning to the spirit world there is the certain knowledge you will see them again, and this knowing will help you through your sadness and grief.

Allow yourself to feel the emotions of separation and passing, there is no shame in this. But recognise if you can, the progress you have made, the strength you have gained, and the ability to love from the heart which has been at the centre of your relationship.

All blessings,
Joseph

Judgement & Acceptance

We often talk to you about the importance of not judging yourself or others, and we would like to explain a little more about why this is so important. Your world is not a world of perfection, everything has flaws or weaknesses, it is the nature of the physical world. You are part of this, you are not expected to be perfect in your physical manifestation, neither is anyone else. The learning is to recognise and accept each other as your are and to replace judgement with compassion and understanding. This does not mean pretending everything is in great harmony and everyone is just wonderful. It means accepting each other in all aspects and offering kindness and love, because it is not for your eyes to see the journey each person is taking.

Do not think we are unaware of the darkness in your world, but we wish to help you to lift your energy vibrations away from that darkness towards the light and the good. Yet still you need to be aware of the forces that are in opposition to the Light, without giving them any room in your approach to life.

This is a deep subject and here we have only touched the surface. Be gentle with yourself and each other, do not expect perfection or for everyone to be like you. To learn to accept and not judge is a challenging earth lesson.

All blessings,
Joseph

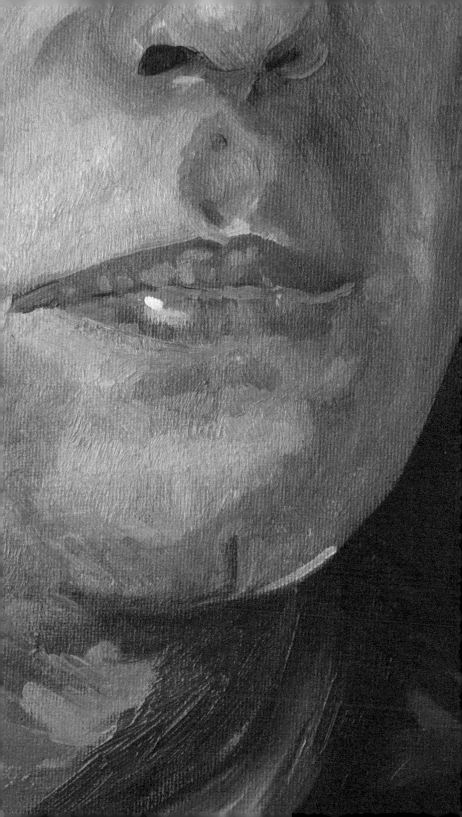

Do Not Give Away Your Power

You are the centre of your universe and this is how it should be. When you allow another to become the centre of your universe you give away your power, you become weak and will stumble. No other person should carry the responsibility of all your hopes and dreams, your happiness is your own responsibility.

Keep a strong core, know your own worth and value, and from this centre give forth love and kindness. This can be a hard lesson, many of you have been in the situation where you have allowed another to dominate your life. The strength and wisdom you have gained from stepping away from this is immeasurable.

We need our Light Army to be strong and you have proved yourself in different ways to be true to the light. We give you our Love and Gratitude for your strength, for returning to your own power and sending forth the light for others.

All blessings,
Joseph

Changing Energies

Understand that the energies surrounding you are shifting and changing in ways you have not experienced before. For this reason you may find yourself acting out of character, and feeling insecure and unbalanced. It is important you do not chastise yourself when this occurs, but allow yourself the freedom to change, to become more aware, more attuned.

Whenever there is change, there is initial uncertainty, but if you quietly accept the changes and your different outlook, then great progress can be made. We love you, we see and understand your difficulties, but rest assured all is happening in the way that will lead you closer to the light.

Accept change, accept that you are evolving with the changing energies, give yourself tolerance and peace.

All blessings,
Joseph

Where You Belong in the Spirit World

When you return to our world and are rested, you automatically gravitate to where you feel most comfortable. To the place that is in harmony with your vibration.

There is no question of you or anyone else going to the wrong spirit home, because the law is perfect, and only those of the same light quality can enter the appropriate place.

Does this sound strange? No matter how well born or lowly born you may be in your earth world, it is the quality of the soul that guides a person back home in our world. Like will be attracted to like.

Imagine a long street where every house and its setting is different. Some will attract, others will not, but you will choose the one where you feel quite at home.

As your energy vibration changes, as you become more charged with light (there is only going forwards here) so you will move to the next place that it is appropriate for you to be. There is nothing haphazard, all souls have their place where they belong.

All blessings,
Joseph

CHANGES (1)

Although many of the structures in your world are undergoing radical change at the moment, and some are ceasing altogether, we would like to reassure you that the reality, the Truth of Spirit never changes. What you are experiencing is the disruption of manmade structures that have outlived their time or that have been founded on greed, not for the benefit of all.

There is much fear being generated at this time, as a way of life that has been familiar to you is undergoing much change, and there is uncertainty of where this will lead. World leaders are caught up in this chaos and few have the strength or the wisdom to lead in this changing world.

We wish to remind you that you carry the unchanging reality within yourself. Do not be fearful or uncertain because you are an infinite spirit created from Love. Whatever happens in your earth world cannot change this. Centre yourself with you inner reality, lean heavily upon the Truth that you know, that is the unchanging love that surrounds you always. Go within and allow this knowledge to bring you peace.

All blessings,
Joseph

Spirit Terminology (Changes 2)

It has been drawn to our attention that some of the terminology we use, while understood by you in essence, is hard for you to incorporate into your everyday way of being. Such terminology is 'go within'. While your heart responds to these words, your mind may ponder 'how do I do that?'

And so we would like to give greater clarity with some of the terminology we use. Your world is full of sound and busyness, your senses are assaulted in all ways in your daily life, even in your own home with the different forms of media. The best way to achieve inner stillness is through the Breath, the rhythm of your breathing, this will instantly bring a feeling of calm and link you with a different reality.

Whatever you are doing, stop for a moment, be still and breathe, become aware of what is beneath the surface, the life that is present in all things. You vibrate with this, you are part of it in your true being. Imagine your daily life as a crust, an outer layer full of activity, beneath this is a stillness that is full of life, that touches and intermingles with everything. This is what we mean by saying 'go within'. Be still, breathe and link with this inner reality. It is not something you need to struggle towards, that requires great effort, rather it is a letting go so that you can rest easy. It is already within you and always will be.

All Blessings,
Joseph

GRACE
(CHANGES 3)

There is a way of being in your earth world where you are absorbed by the everyday circumstances and emotions that surround you, but there is also a way of being, where just for a few minutes, you rise above this and life seems to flow, all is well, you are in harmony with your life.

It is like a state of Grace, in that moment all is balanced, you have been given a glimpse of your true spiritual reality and life as it is lived away from the physical plane. Perhaps this may occur in a dream or in your physical life, it is a perfect moment. Treasure these moments, they will lead you to an understanding of the harmony that exists between all forms of created life, all worlds, all universes. Everything breathes, everything is linked. Divine Breath breathes life into every life form.

Feel at one with all that surrounds you for this is the Truth. You share the breath of life with the trees, the earth, all peoples and animals wherever they may come from.

All blessings, Joseph

ARTWORK BY KATY JONES

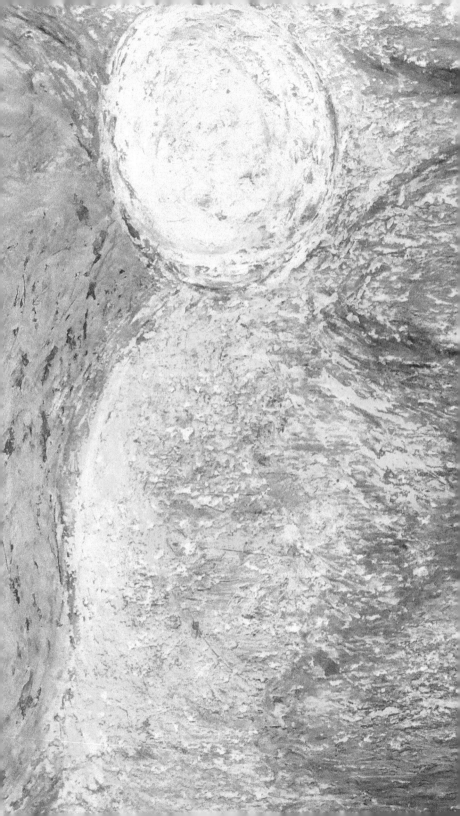

The Silent Army

You may wonder my friends what you can do in a practical manner that will help alleviate the suffering and chaos in the world at this time. There are some that are called to travel to the places of suffering with their skills, but this is not for everyone. As you all know, all life is energy, and energy is a power you all possess. It is how you use that power that can make a difference in your world.

Once you are aware of this power which each one of you possesses you cannot 'unknow' it, so it is important that your thoughts and actions reflect not judgement, not fear, but trust in the goodness of life. This may seem ridiculous in the face of what is occurring in your world at this time, but nevertheless, to turn your thoughts always to that which is positive, is not judgemental and is for the benefit of all living beings is the greatest gift you can give to help the balance in your earth world.

We cannot stress too much the strength of the power of thought, it is like a silent army working either to undermine or to uplift. Always look to the light, to the positive, take the loving and kind option both in your thoughts and your deeds. Let your silent army be the one that brings peace and harmony, simplicity and trust.

All blessings,
Joseph

Dark Moments

Do not shy away from the dark moments in life, either your own, or those of the people you know. Instead face them and take the candle of light which you carry always, into that dark moment. Always the light will illumine the darkness.

Blessings,
Joseph

Forgiving

Dear Child of the Universe, we would like to speak to you this day about forgiveness. Is it not forgiving your loved ones which allows and helps you to live from one day to the next? Without forgiveness you would struggle to move forward in your life.

It is having the courage to forgive which makes you the person who sees from a higher perspective. It is true forgiveness which helps you to thrive. When you decide to forgive another, you are not saying that you have understood or approved of another's behaviour but you are acknowledging that no human behaves in a perfect way all of the time. You would not learn without making mistakes. Mistakes help you to grow spiritually within the confines of a human body. Well done for the forgiveness you have achieved so far on your life journey. Blessed be. Amen.

Channelled by Linda Peters
7th June 2021

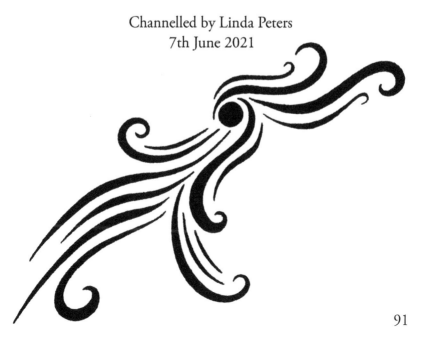

Truth

(Morning following eclipse and super Moon)

Dear Higher Self, great Spirit, Angels, Spirit guides and spiritual helpers, what would you like to say to us today please?

Dear people of the earth, today we would like to speak to you about truth. Being true to yourself and of speaking the truth. It can be a habit to tell casual lies and by that we mean untruths which you may consider unimportant. But what is your soul feeling when it witnesses these untruths? It becomes detached from you and moves further and further away from your alignment.

We would like to make a suggestion to you, dear ones, strive to stay aligned with your true higher self, by this we mean behaving in ways which keep you connected with your spirit self, your inner being. To keep aligned with high vibrational behaviour we suggest being truthful, sensitive to others, being helpful, kind, knowledgeable, wise, understanding, unselfish, undemanding, and caring.

Walk in nature, take time to be in silence every day (meditation) or any spiritual practice which you enjoy; it does not need to be for hours, just take the rest time when you need it. Keep your thoughts about yourself and others positive (high vibrational).

Gossip, negative thoughts and anger keep your vibrational frequency low and dense. Refrain from judgement, dear ones. This is not the way, not the answer. We will speak more about truth at another time. Blessings to you. Amen

Channelled by Linda Peters
27th May 2021

YOU ARE A SPIRIT IN A PHYSICAL BODY

You are an infinite spirit. You take on a role, you put on a body-like a suit of clothing when you incarnate to the earth plane, but this is designed to help you in your spiritual development. All people are different and yet all the same. This is a difficult paradox to understand, but the realisation would prevent much of the violence, bitterness and hatred in your world.

Wars are generated from people believing they are different to one another. Of a different race, a different religion or a different colour. However these things are only superficial, they are the costume that the spirit has chosen to wear in a particular incarnation.

All are spirit, all are moving forwards towards the Light in their different ways. This is why it is called the Brotherhood of Man, because you are all brothers and sisters coming from the same Source. Each of you carries your own cross, sometimes visible, sometimes not, but look beneath the veneer and reach out to the spirit in each person. You are all here to help each other forwards.

All blessings,
Joseph

Religion

There are many religions in your world that are built up with many words, many instructions about how to behave, what is Truth and what is not. These religions have been formed for some reasons that are beneficial to mankind and some that are not. To belong to a group of people with the same beliefs is comforting, it gives a feeling of belonging, and the energy of worship is much stronger. However, religions were also founded for reasons of power and control, and this has caused many problems.

What we would like to say to you is this. You are all part of God, every soul has the God Spirit within, so your path to the Light, to God, is within each and every one of you. You do not need to be told what to believe, what rules to follow, what is right and what is wrong. All you need is right there in your heart, and it is encompassed by the word Love. To treat all livings beings, all forms of life with loving kindness as if they were a part of yourself, as indeed they are.

The times and energies of earth life are changing. Organised religions are no longer holding the influence and power that they used to. Some are being used for destructive purposes that have nothing to do with their original intent. Each person is a part of God, they must follow the dictates of their own heart to know what is right and wrong. It is good to join with others who look to the Light for the Light then becomes stronger than you can possibly imagine, but do it from your own hearts, your own inner knowing, not because it is the correct form of belief.

It is all so simple. Treat all with Love and understanding, and have joy in your heart that you are spreading the Light, a reflection of the Great Love your Heavenly Father has for you.

All blessings,
Joseph

Artwork by Linda Peters

Moving Forwards

Sometimes, you will set yourself goals on your spiritual journey. You may think "Maybe if I could just see the Spirit World and those that dwell there, or hear the voices of my Guides, or perform miraculous healing, THEN I would be achieving my spiritual goals." But when one peak is reached, it is only a plateau and the journey never ends. That is what is so wonderful. There are no external goals, only the gentle going forwards from within, the opening of the spiritual flower of your inner knowing.

It is not so much about your spiritual abilities, but the unfolding of love from within your heart. It does not matter how gifted you are as a medium or healer, it is the joy of service that is important, the giving of yourself to allow the loving spirit within you to shine and to offer help and assistance to all living beings.

The spiritual path unfolds gradually and steadily, it is different for each and every one of you. Each has their own destiny to fulfil, the purpose for which you have incarnated, do not try to be what it is not in your nature to be. Just allow yourself to unfold in the way that is right for you, not for anyone else. Do not be told how you should or should not be, only you know your path, it is written in your heart, in your spirit, it is the reason why you incarnated. Trust yourself, trust your spirit guides, allow the truth within you to shine and guide you.

You have an inner light, and as you link with the light and love of spirit this will shine brighter and brighter and you will know without doubt the way to go forwards. Follow your own inner guidance, it will not let your down.

All Blessings,
Joseph

Fearful

Greetings Children of the Earth. We come to you this day with words and vibrations of hope from all. When you decided you would incarnate on Earth in a physical body you were inspired and excited to make a positive change to the Collective, to make your Mark, in the absence of fear.

We would like to remind you of this, because fear, dear ones, is not the way forward. Fear prevents you from being who you truly are, prevents your light from shining out to the world and prevents you from completing your goal.

Love is the only way, dear ones. Love is always the answer, whoever you are dealing with, let love light your decisions and surround your actions, for with love as your priority you are staying on your chosen pathway. Make every word, every decision every thought and every action come from love. This is the way forward for you, dear one. Blessed Be.

Channelled by Linda Peters
23rd May 2021

Artwork by Katy Jones

LOVE

Dear Spirit Angels, Higher Self,

We rejoice in the service you provide today and that you have come to meet with us. At this moment in time we would like to speak with you about love. It is a word which is used widely and regularly in your Earth and how many think of its true meaning? To love is not to judge, but to accept. To love is not to ridicule but to rejoice in someone else's joy. To love is not to feel jealousy, feel sad, or to feel apart from the world. We bring our love to each and every one of you today and every day and encourage you individually to explore the feeling of love in its true essence.

Practice loving every one and every thing. Accepting that, even if you are not loving the way another is expressing themselves, feel glad that they are expressing, accepting and understanding that it is okay for them to be and feel differently from you. You are tired now. Rest. Blessings to all. Amen

Channelled by Linda Peters
4th June 2020

ATTACHMENT

You will find that when the energies are challenging on a global scale so this energy is often imprinted on your personal life as well. Things you have relied on in the past that have given you security are no longer there or people who have been a treasured part of your life seem to slip away. Always remember that nothing stays the same, it is the nature of life to develop, to change, to always be moving forwards.

The trick is not to become too attached to any way of life or being so that you wish to keep it always the same. This is impossible, energy must move by its very nature, people you love are never lost to you, you know this, and security is only to be found within yourself, it cannot be relied upon in the ever changing physical world.

So we would ask you to take a lighter approach to life. By this we mean enjoy all that is offered at each moment without trying to hang on to the status quo. All things must change, be like a surfer riding the waves, treasure each moment of experience knowing that the core of all life is love, is eternal life, and rest in the knowledge that you are loved and protected and always will be.

All blessings,
Joseph

LISTENING

When you wish to calm your mind and find inner peace, just listen. Wherever you are, whatever you are doing, especially if you are in the natural world, just stand still and listen. At first you will hear only the sounds that are close by, but gradually you will become aware of sounds in the distance until your whole being is absorbed in the listening. This will bring a feeling of calm because your mind has ceased it restless thoughts and your awareness expands outwards. This is a technique you can use anywhere at any time, and only needs a few minutes. Even listening to the silence can bring great peace.

All blessings,
Joseph

My Father

My father came close when I was meditating one day. He died in 1987. I asked him what was the most important thing he had learned since being in the Spirit World.

He said "Don't judge yourselves or anyone else, because on earth we can never see the whole picture. Always give compassion and understanding, everyone carries their own cross."

Purpose Of Earth Life

You are often being told that earth life is a school, you are here to learn, to overcome mistakes from the past, to progress spiritually. This is all very well, but sometimes you must wonder why you are learning these lessons, where exactly are you meant to be going?

Sometimes it seems to you that earth life is overcoming one hurdle after another, and where is it all leading, what is the spiritual goal? Imagine that you are a centre of light energy, a pure bright light that has been covered by different layers of clothing. Every time you take a step forwards on your spiritual path an item or layer of clothing falls to the ground, and your light shines brighter. What is the purpose of your light shining brighter you may ask, where does it all lead? It leads to becoming who you truly are, a part of the great shining light of God of our Creator, and this brings such joy that it cannot be described.

You may wonder if you actually want to stop being "you" and merge with the light of love, but we would re-assure you that your consciousness remains, you just lose the trappings that tie you down to a lower vibration. Many have caught glimpses of this feeling of joy, this merging with the higher vibration of light, and it is these glimpses that help you to keep faith, to keep moving forwards along your spiritual path. Indeed there is no other way in truth, for to return to the Source of all Love is written within your heart, it is as natural as breathing, an inner knowing of where you truly belong.

We are all part of the some journey, but we take different paths depending on our inner being and the way we have chosen to progress. This is why it is so important to always reach out a helping hand to those around you, for truly we are all on the same journey, there is no separation.

All blessings,
Joseph

ARTWORK BY LINDA PETERS

SHINE

Spirit Angelic Beings, what words of love do you have for us today?

Greetings Earth people, it is wonderful to make your acquaintance this day, in May 2021 of your Earth Time. We are the light beings of the seventh angelic realm and we come to you in peace. We love and support you all individually and as a collective. Dear Child, of your wonderful earth now is the time for you to be yourself and shine, spread your wings by taking every opportunity that comes your way. Be the Light that shines brightly within you and pass it on to those around you. Listen to your inner voice and always be true to yourself. We love and support each and everyone of you. Blessed Be.

Channelled by Linda Peters
21st May 2021

About the Authors & Artists

Kathalyn Hamilton

Kathalyn has been working with Spirit for nearly 40 years, both as a healer and a medium. In 1992, she qualified as an astrologer and finds it endlessly fascinating. To keep her feet on the ground, she loves gardening and walking her two slightly loopy dogs in the woods. She and Linda met at Roger's development circle about 6 years ago and found they worked well together and shared a love of linking with the Spirit World and the Angels. Kathalyn and Joseph were together in incarnation in the Middle East at the time of Jesus and have been working together in this incarnation for many years.

Linda Peters

Linda has been working with Spirit since visiting the Point of Light Spiritual group in 2010, but she will tell you that she has been talking to Angels since about 1990. Back in the early nineties there wasn't a huge section of any book shop devoted to Mind Body Spirit books, but thanks to Diana Cooper, Linda realised how being aware of the Angels enhanced her life.

It was whilst visiting the Point of Light in Monmouth that Linda met Dawn, Roger and Beryl, and Roger suggested that Linda could be a psychic artist. Since then spirit/psychic art, mediumship and healing have been a way of life for Linda, developing her skills at Roger's weekly Spiritual Development classes and working regularly at Mind Body Spirit events on her own and then eventually teaming up with Kathalyn. Linda's spirit artist signs his name RAMA but other artists also 'visit' with RAMA's permission. Her relationship with her guide RAMA is always evolving and changing and it never ceases to amaze Linda how spirit manage to connect with us.

Regarding the images in this book, Linda has asked Spirit and the Angels to enfold you in their love and healing light and for you to receive exactly what you need at any given time.

www.artistlindapeters.com

Facebook group: Spirit Art Angels

Katy Jones

Katy is a mother, daughter, sister, friend, primary school teacher, medium, channeller, healer, healing counsellor, artist, empowerment and awareness coach, house sitter, explorer, animal and nature lover and much more to be discovered. She started channelling art and words in 2015, it gives her much pleasure.

Katy feels very blessed to be able to access a beautiful, peaceful state and share such creativity and spiritual guidance. Her council of guides, Majestic Infinite would like everyone to live knowing that all there is is love; unconditional love, a love without any judgement.

Katy feels it is her soul's journey to empower, guide and inspire individuals to be authentic and for them to discover their infinite powers from within. Katy would like to extend great thanks to Kate and Linda for such a wonderful opportunity to contribute and share the work of Mez, a collection of light workers who choose to work with her.

More information on Katy's work can be found at infinitepowersfromwithin.com

Hazel Burridge

Hazel is from Wales but now spends her time between Cornwall and Gloucestershire. Recently her work has included designing shop window displays and tattoo design, but her greatest love is interior design. Her free time is spent paddle boarding, kayaking and swimming.

Lightning Source UK Ltd.
Milton Keynes UK
UKHW051341161022
410538UK00001B/1